Look After Yourself

Activity Book

Introduction

This activity book is based upon the **Look After Yourself** programmes from Channel 4 Schools for Early Years.

It offers ideas and activities that will be useful in supporting programmes in the **Look After Yourself** unit. They may also be used independently.

Developed for use in the classroom with Early Years children, the resource offers a range of activities differentiated to meet the learning needs of children of mixed abilities.

The activities broadly develop personal, social and health education, but concentrate in particular on language, literacy, numeracy and science. Some of the activities are designed to involve parents in their child's learning.

Health Education

Health Education is an important part of the personal and social development of young children. It provides opportunities for children to develop their knowledge of, and understanding about, healthy lifestyles. This is vital if children are to make choices and decisions about their own health in the future.

In order for children to make decisions, they need opportunities to examine their existing knowledge about health, and to explore their attitudes, relationships and feelings towards themselves and others. Involving children in their own learning through activities and discussion, as developed in this activity book, will encourage them to build on the existing knowledge that they bring with them to school and to make healthier choices as they grow.

Contents

Keep Clean

Activity sheet 1.
When I get up

The activity

Ask the children to describe what they do when they get ready for school. Discuss the order in which they do these activities, emphasising healthy aspects like brushing their teeth. Give each child a copy of the activity sheet. They should cut out the nine pictures and then sequence them to tell the story. Young children could do this as a group activity. Older children could draw their own pictures and write a sentence.

Further activities

Use a clock to tell the story using time: 'I get up at..., have a wash at... and get dressed at...'.

Activity sheet 2.
What to wear

The activity

Understanding the need to wear appropriate and clean clothing is an important part of personal hygiene and well-being. Show pictures of people wearing clothing suitable to specific types of weather and activities, such as a chef and a person on the beach in summer. Ask the children to say why the clothing is appropriate. Distribute the activity sheet and ask them to match the appropriate item of clothing in the picture with the activity.

Further activities

Discuss why it is that we wash ourselves and why clothes are changed and washed regularly. What is it that washing actually does? Focus also on the sense of 'feeling good' that washing and wearing clean clothes promotes.

Activity sheet 3.
Germs

The activity

Children can be taught about hygiene and the relationship this has to feeling well or unwell. Explain that germs can't be seen without a microscope and that they can make us unwell. Discuss how germs are spread: for example by eating food with unwashed hands, not washing hands after having been to the toilet, eating food that has been on the floor, flies landing on food, and coughing and sneezing over food or people. Ask them to complete the activity sheet by drawing lines between the two sets of pictures.

Further activities

Discuss the jobs that are done in the home to keep it clean: washing clothes, vacuuming, cleaning toilets and so on. Discuss who does these jobs and why they are necessary.

Activity sheet 4.
Washing your hands

The activity

Children should learn that they have to take responsibility for themselves. Good health education is about enabling children to make healthy choices and decisions. Ask them to say how they look after themselves at home and at school, such as by washing, brushing their teeth, dressing themselves, tying their laces, combing their hair, feeding themselves, turning on lights and flushing the toilet. Give them the activity sheet and ask them to complete it.

Further activities

Review the reasons for keeping personally clean. Name all the times when it is necessary to wash our hands.

Activity sheet 5.
Cuts and grazes

The activity

Children of all ages have experienced minor cuts and grazes. Discuss why washing and cleaning cuts and grazes is important in preventing germs from getting into our bodies and causing infections. Give out the activity sheet and ask them to match the words in the pictures with the spaces in the crossword, then use the words to make a sentence in the boxes beneath.

Further activities

Discuss why we need skin, why we need to keep it clean and how to do this.

Activity sheet 6.
Keep clean check list

The activity

Remind the children about germs and how important it is to take preventative action and especially to keep clean. Remind them that germs are tiny creatures called microbes or bacteria. Good bacteria (antibodies) are those that help fight illnesses caused by harmful bacteria (viruses). Harmful bacteria enter the body in a variety of ways. Talk about the need to wash regularly, especially after having been to the toilet, and to make sure that our germs don't spread to other people. Invite them to take the activity sheet home and complete it for a week.

Further activities

Ask the children to list all the things that can be done to keep harmful bacteria out of the home, our clothes and ourselves. Turn the results into suggested rules for keeping clean.

When I get up

Name _____

Cut out the pictures and put them in the right order to make a story.

10 on coloured A3.

What to wear

Name

Finish each sentence by choosing the right piece of clothing from the list.

When jumping in puddles, wear........................ .

When going for a swim, wear a ....

When in bed, wear........................ .

When playing in the snow, wear........................ .

After a bath, put on clean ....

When skipping, wear........................ .

wellies

PE kit

gloves

swimming costume

pyjamas

pants and vest

Early Years: **Look After Yourself**

Germs

Name _____

Look at the pictures on the top row. What should be done next?
Draw a line to link the pictures.

Atchoo!!!

ICE CREAM

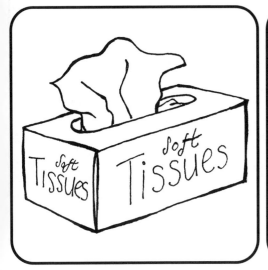

Soft Tissues

CLINGFILM

Washing your hands

Name

Draw a smiley face if you agree.

You should wash your hands

before you eat.

You should wash your hands

after watching television.

You should wash your hands

after playing in the sandpit.

You should wash your hands

after going to the toilet.

You should wash your hands

before riding your bike.

You should wash your hands

after stroking animals.

Now finish this sentence.
I think it is important to wash my hands often because ....

Early Years: **Look After Yourself**

© 1998 Channel Four Learning Limited

Cuts and grazes

Name

Put the words in the pictures in the right place in the crossword.

cold

cuts

wash

water

with

Now write the words in a sentence,
using the boxes below.

Early Years: **Look After Yourself**

© 1998 Channel Four Learning Limited

Keep clean check list

Fill in the missing words. Use this list and keep a record of what you do each day to stay clean.

Put a ✓

Monday	Tuesday	Wednesday	Thursday	Friday

When I get up in the ...., I must have a wash, a shower or a ....

Then I must clean my .... and brush my ....

I must wash my hands before I ...., especially if I have been to the ....

When I cut myself, I must .... the cut and cover it with a ....

I must not eat .... that has been dropped on the ....

When I .... I must use a handkerchief, so that my .... don't spread to everyone else.

Early Years: **Look After Yourself**

Eat Well

Activity sheet 1.
Which foods?

The activity
Children need to be aware of the wide range of foods and understand that they need to eat different foods to be healthy. What do they eat at home? Give out the activity sheet and discuss the foods shown. Do they come from plants or animals? Ask the children to write each name in the space provided. Count how many examples of each food are shown. Let them cut up the pictures and stick them in number order on to a piece of paper.

Further activities.
Ask the children to bring in labels from different foods used at home. Classify where they come from.

Activity sheet 2.
My favourite meal

The activity
Eating healthily requires some knowledge about foods. Explain that food from animals gives us protein to help us grow (there may be vegetarians in the class, so be diplomatic); food from the vegetable/cereal group from plants gives us energy; fruit contains vitamins to ward off colds and flu. Which foods do we need less of? Why should we eat fewer cakes and sweets? Using the activity sheet, discuss which foods from each group are their favourites. Tell them to draw and colour each example on the plate and label them. Ask them to say what it is about their favourite foods they like. This sheet could be taken home and parents might help the children complete it.

Further activities.
Use the information from the activity sheet to create simple histograms of favourite foods in each food group.

Activity sheet 3.
The party tree

The activity
Children need to know that food is vital for energy and growth, although the most tempting foods contain the most sugars and can, if eaten to excess, have undermining consequences for health, particularly in terms of weight gain and dental decay. Ask the children to collect the wrappers of all their favourite foods and categorise them (vegetables, sweets, fruits, cereals, dairy products). Which is the most popular category? Talk about what happens to teeth that are brushed infrequently and the consequences of too much sugar on teeth. Ask the children to complete the activity sheet.

Further activities
Follow up the completed sheet by identifying with the children all those foods containing hidden sugars.

Activity sheet 4.
How do they taste?

The activity
Children often won't try new foods because they are not in their experience. Ask the class to describe how different foods taste. Provide different foods and ask them to predict how they will taste. Ensure that the foods shown in the activity sheet are included. Invite them to taste each food and choose a word that best describes the taste. Discuss which tastes they liked and those they did not. Ask the children to complete the activity sheet.

Further activities
Introduce different foods. Blindfold the children so that they cannot see the food they are tasting. Can they identify the food? Can they identify the taste?

Activity sheet 5.
Drink up!

The activity
Children need to know the importance of drinking liquids. Tell them that about three-quarters of the weight of our body is made up of water. What might happen if we sweat a lot? Tell them that we cannot live for long without drinking. Conduct a survey on favourite drinks and use the data to complete the activity sheet.

Further activities
Find out what and how much each child drinks during the day. This could be completed at home as a 'drinks diary'.

Activity sheet 6.
Containers

The activity
Explain that food labels often give not only the name but also information about the nutritional value of the food. Tell them that containers enable food to be kept fresh for a long time. Collect some containers – what information can be found – a name, picture clue, producer? Use this information to help them complete the activity sheet.

Further activities
What might happen if food is not kept in a container? Leave out a slice of bread overnight and keep another slice wrapped up. Do all foods need to be kept in containers? For example, do nuts need to be kept in a container? What happens to apples when they are left for a long time? Are there different rates of deterioration for different foods? Does the skin or casing of a food act as a means of keeping food fresh?

Which foods?

Complete the names of the foods under the pictures.

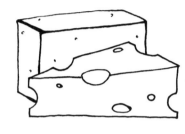

ca _ r _ _ s   ch _ _ k _ _   br _ a _   c _ _ _ s   ch _ _ _ e

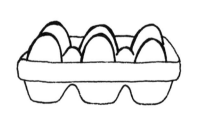

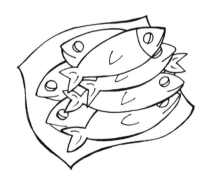

e _ g _   p _ _ a _ _ e _   f _ _ _   m _ _ _   b _ n _ _ _ s

Early Years: **Look After Yourself**

My favourite meal

Name ....

Draw and colour your favourite food on the plate.

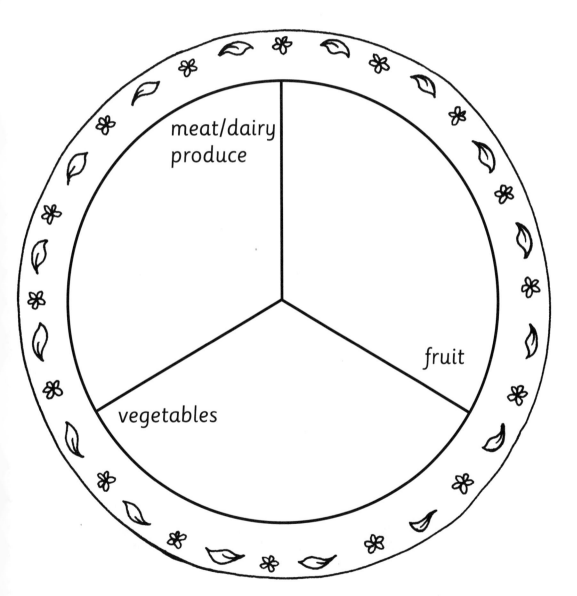

My favourite food is ....

A new food I tasted was ....

It is from the .... group.

It tasted ....

Next, I want to try ....

Early Years: **Look After Yourself**

© 1998 Channel Four Learning Limited

The party tree

Name

Which foods on the tree have not had sugar added?
Draw them in the picnic basket. Label your drawing.

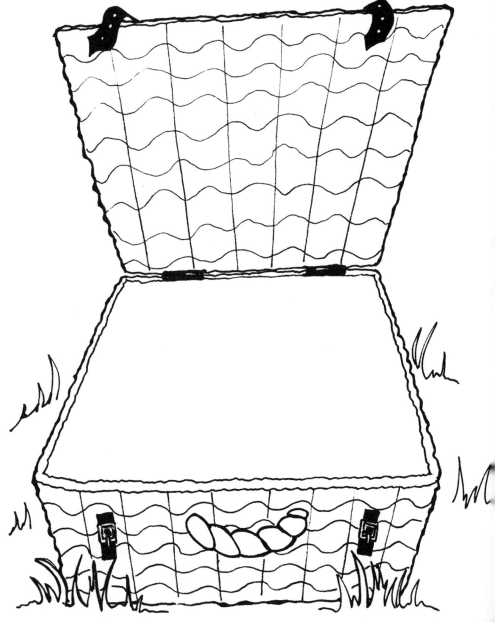

Early Years: **Look After Yourself**

© 1998 Channel Four Learning Limited

How do they taste?

Choose a word from the word box to describe these foods.

The apple tastes ....

The sugar tastes ....

The chilli tastes ....

The coffee tastes ....

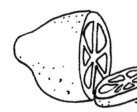

The lemon tastes ....

The crisps taste ....

| sweet | salty | sour | bitter | spicy |

Drink up!

Ask the other children in your class to tell you their favourite drink. Write each total in the box by the picture.

tea

fruit juice

milk

fizzy pop

water

coffee

milk shake

hot chocolate

Early Years: **Look After Yourself**

Containers

What drink or food do you think is in each container? Design labels for each one, giving information on what it contains.

a drink carton

a jar

a tin

a plastic container

a packet

a box carton

Keep Fit

Activity sheet 1.
Having fun

The activity
Talk with the children about the different types of activities they participate in which count as exercise. Which are they good at and which do they enjoy the most? Are there any they cannot do but would like to be able to do? Distribute and talk about the activity sheet. Ask them to colour in the activities they enjoy doing and then write a sentence about the one they enjoy the most.

Further activities
Ask the children to draw histograms of favourite exercise activities and find out what people at home enjoyed doing when they were young.

Activity sheet 2.
How do they feel?

The activity
For exercise to be beneficial, children need to get warm and out of breath for at least 20 minutes three times a week. Ask them how they feel when they have exercised. Do they feel hot and sweaty, out of breath, tired, happy or thirsty? Are their hearts beating fast? Ask them to match the picture with the appropriate word on the activity sheet. Discuss why exercise is important, and why we need food for energy and liquids to replace the sweat. Talk about the need for sleep – it allows time for the body to repair itself and is when we do most of our growing.

Further activities
In PE, have the children participate in a range of activities and then stop them and ask them how they feel. Reflect on what they have learned about exercise.

Activity sheet 3.
Puffed and chuffed

The activity
Children should know that physical activities help us stay healthy and also cause a variety of feelings (such as happiness, fear, anger and disappointment) as well as physical change, such as breathlessness and tiredness. What happens to the body when it is very busy? Focus on breathing, sweating and aching. Give out the activity sheet. Point out that some of the answers may say whether a person feels good or satisfied, as well as how their body feels and may react.

Further activities
Ask the children to draw a picture of their favourite game, showing the parts of their body that they move, special clothes they might wear and any equipment needed.

Activity sheet 4.
Places to keep fit

The activity
It is important that children are taught to exercise in appropriate and safe places. Discuss the games they play at school and at home, how many people are required for the games, the amount of space needed and what determines how much space is needed. Discuss where, in their own locality, is the best place to play each game and why. Invite the children to complete the activity sheet.

Further activity
Working in groups, invite the children to make up a set of simple rules about where to play in safety and with satisfaction.

Activity sheet 5.
Name the joints

The activity
Children should become increasingly aware of some of the health benefits of exercise. During PE or games, tell them to go floppy as if they had no bones, then go stiff and unable to move their joints. Ask them to run, skip, hop and jump and to then identify which joints they used. Write the names of these on the board. Invite them to write the name for each joint in the appropriate space on the activity sheet. Send the activity sheet home for parents to cut up and play a game (beetle drive) using the numbered body parts and a dice. The winner is the first to collect the complete body.

Further activities
The puppet outline may also be used for naming other parts of the body or to create a simple puppet.

Activity sheet 6.
Dressing up

The activity
Freedom of movement, hygiene and safety are all essential reasons for wearing appropriate clothing during physical activity. Discuss the different clothing worn for sports and why clothing for one sport might not be worn for another. Give out the activity sheet.

Further activities
Consider when else we wear clothes for different occasions and different seasons. Reflect on the relevance of gender differences and identity.

Having fun

Colour in the pictures of those activities you enjoy doing.

How do they feel?

Name _____

Choose a word from below to match each picture.
Draw a line from the word to the picture.

| happy | hungry | tired | hot | breathless |

Early Years: **Look After Yourself**
© 1998 Channel Four Learning Limited

Puffed and chuffed

Name

Look at the pictures. Choose a word from the word box to explain how the children may be feeling.

When Jaspal swims he feels..........................

When Olivia plays hopscotch she feels..........................

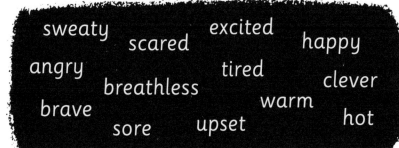

sweaty   excited   happy

scared

angry   tired

breathless   clever

brave   warm

sore   upset   hot

When Eddie skips he feels.........................

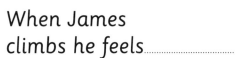

When Lara rides a bike she feels.........................

When James climbs he feels.........................

When Kate and John chase each other they feel.........................

Early Years: **Look After Yourself**

Places to keep fit

Name

Draw a line from each group of people to the places they can go to keep fit.
Complete the sentence in each box.

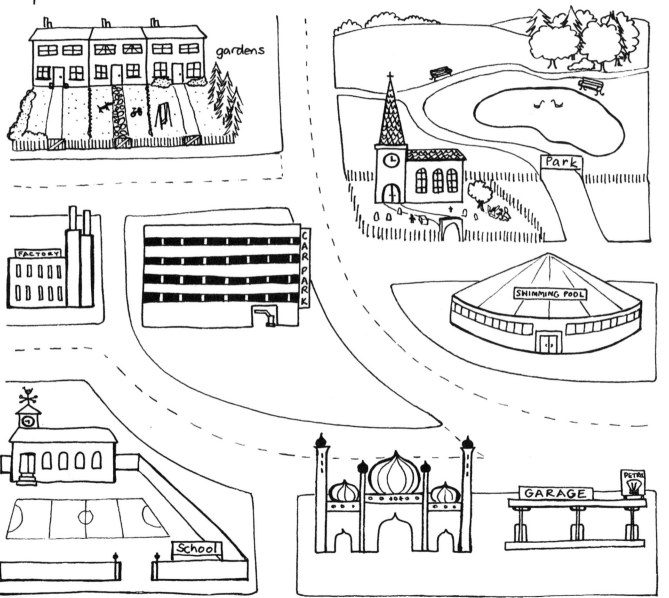

Friends can keep fit ....

Families can keep fit ....

Classmates can keep fit ....

Early Years: **Look After Yourself**

© 1998 Channel Four Learning Limited

Name the joints

Activity sheet 5

Complete the labels of the joints. Cut out the pieces to make a puppet or play a game.

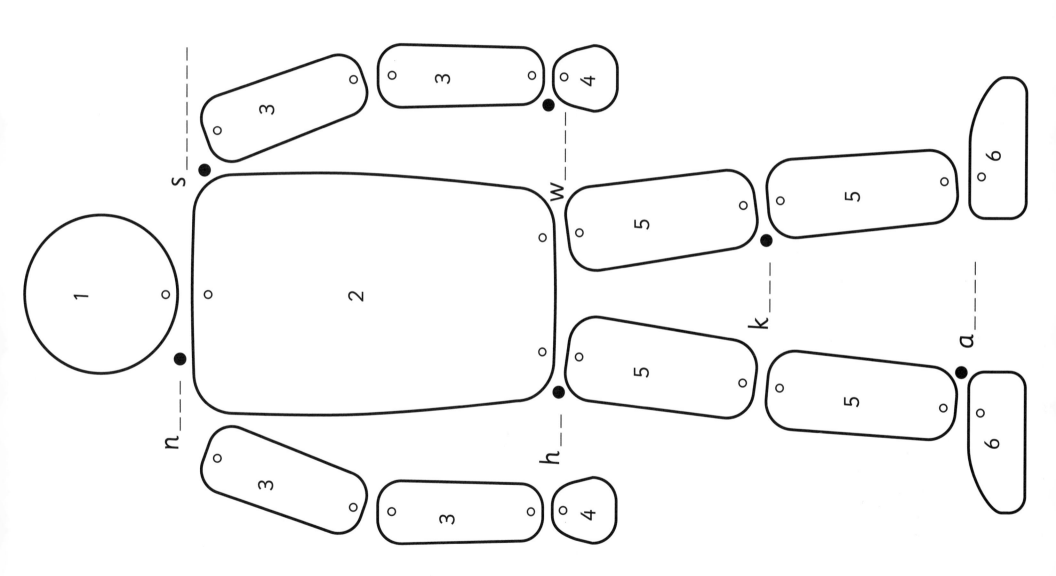

Early Years: **Look After Yourself**

© 1998 Channel Four Learning Limited

Dressing up

Izzy has put on four different kinds of clothes for different types of exercise.
Match the activity to the clothing by drawing a line. Say what each activity
is and complete the words.

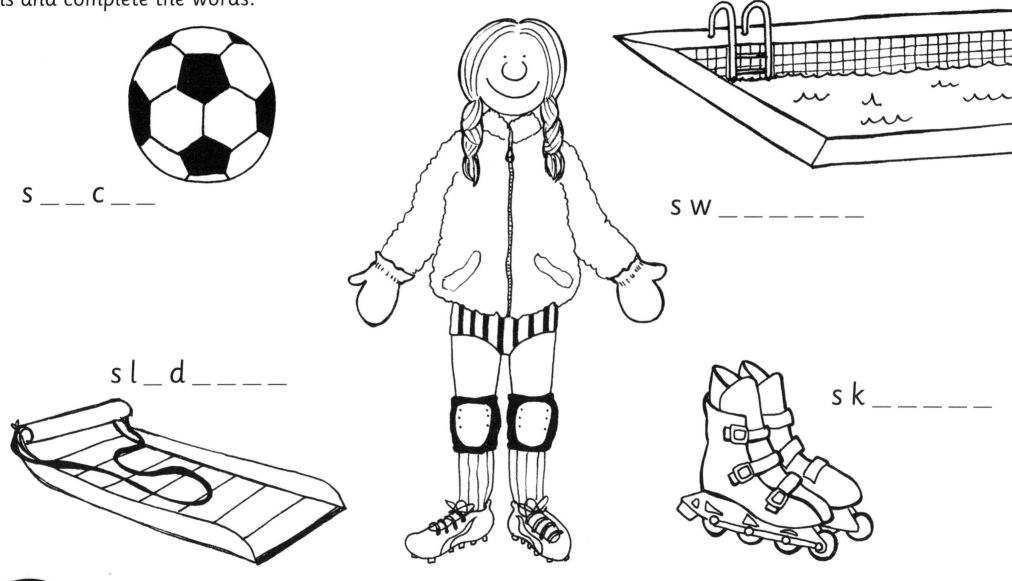

s _ _ c _ _

s w _ _ _ _ _ _

s l _ d _ _ _ _

s k _ _ _ _ _

Early Years: **Look After Yourself**

© 1998 Channel Four Learning Limited

Keep Safe

Activity sheet 1.
Feeling safe

The activity

Children need to be aware of what makes them feel unsafe or frightened and to know how to keep safe and find help. Ask them to say what things make them feel unsafe or even frightened – tell them those things which frighten you. Before asking them to complete the activity sheet, discuss the examples shown. For each set, ask them to draw a picture of another situation and to label it.

Further activities

Create a display of their pictures and sentences under the headings of 'Things that frighten us', 'People we feel safe with' and 'Places where we feel safe'. Discuss who the children should tell if they ever feel frightened or unsafe.

Activity sheet 2.
Use your senses

The activity

Children should be aware of the potential dangers in the local and immediate environment. Using the senses is a good way to protect ourselves. Test the children's knowledge with simple questions, such as: How do we know when something is hot? What might tell us that something isn't safe to drink? How do we know when it is safe to cross the road? What could tell us that something should not be touched? Now ask them to complete the activity sheet.

Further activities

Consider with the class that even babies use their senses to know about, and respond to, things in their daily routine. Discuss with the class the likely daily routine of a baby and which senses babies might use for finding out about things that affect them in their lives.

Activity sheet 3.
Safely home

The activity

Children must know of potential dangers in the local environment. Discuss the dangers associated with the road. List their suggestions. Do the same with dangers in the home and garden. Ask the children to complete the activity sheet. Compare the seven dangerous items on the sheet with those the class has listed. Are all accounted for?

Further activities

Consider whether potential hazards exist in the school. As a class, conduct a safety audit starting in the classroom.

Activity sheet 4.
Signs

The activity

Children should be aware of signs and respond to them when appropriate. Show them a range of road signs (from the Highway Code or by taking them for a walk around the community). Explain the following information:

* A red circle sign tells us not to do something.

* A red triangle is a warning sign.

* A blue rectangle tells us something we need to know.

* A green rectangle gives us directions.

Using the activity sheet, ask the children to make up their own signs for use around the home or at school.

Further activities

Split the class into four groups: 'Red Circles', 'Red Triangles', 'Blue Rectangles' and 'Green Rectangles'. Ask each person in the group to say something to the others according to the function of the sign they represent. For example, Red Circles might say, 'Don't cross the road from behind a parked car.'

Activity sheet 5.
Crossing the road safely

The activity

Children need to understand the risks associated with crossing the road and learn how to cross safely. Tell them about the Green Cross Code and together look at the pictures on the activity sheet. Send the activity sheet home and ask parents to go over it with their children.

Further activities

Provide coloured paper, including fluorescent colours, and ask the children to sort them into those which may be more clearly seen in daylight and at night. Which emergency services use these colours? Why? Make pictures of road scenes and safe crossing places.

Activity sheet 6.
Play safely

The activity

Distribute the activity sheet. Ask the children to tick those pictures which show safe places to play or do things and to put a cross by those which do not. For each picture and situation, talk about whether the activity is safe or unsafe. Discuss the fact that playing on swings is safe only if we use them properly. Talk about what the children think might happen in each situation. What should the person do in each case to be safer? What should they do if they see another child in this situation? Who might they tell? Ask the children to choose one 'unsafe' situation, write a safe play slogan for it, such as 'Don't play football in the road', and draw and colour a picture of their own.

Further activities

Take the children out into their community and look at safe and unsafe places to play.

Feeling safe

Finish each sentence. Draw and label another example in each box.

 spiders    dogs    crossing the road

I am frightened of.. .

 family    teacher    pet

I feel safe with my.. .

 in bed    at home    at school

I feel safe when I am.. .

Early Years: **Look After Yourself**

Use your senses

Name

Look at the pictures. Each item could be dangerous if care is not taken.
Link each label to a picture.

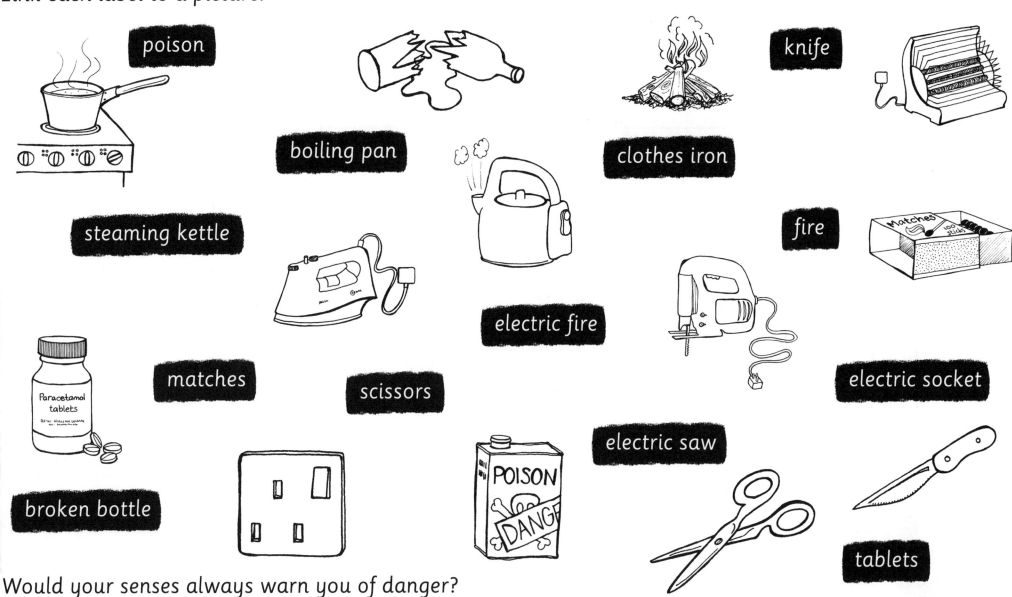

poison

boiling pan

steaming kettle

electric fire

matches

scissors

broken bottle

knife

clothes iron

fire

electric socket

electric saw

tablets

Paracetamol tablets

POISON
DANGE

Would your senses always warn you of danger?

Early Years: **Look After Yourself**

© 1998 Channel Four Learning Limited

Safely home

Name

Draw a line through the maze from Start to Home, avoiding the seven dangers.
As you avoid each danger, write its name in one of the boxes.

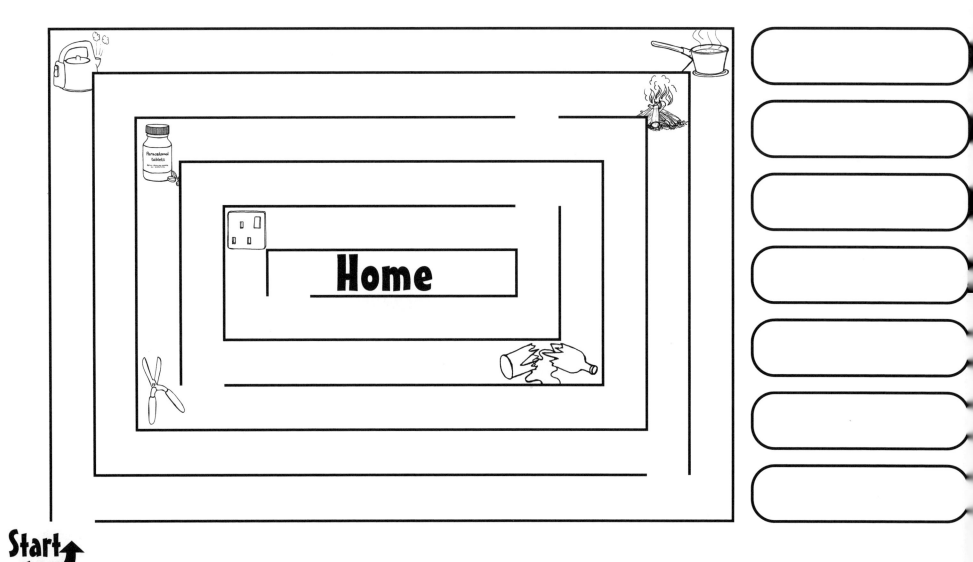

Early Years: **Look After Yourself**

© 1998 Channel Four Learning Limited

Signs

Name

Colour in the signs below. In the middle of each sign say what it could say to help us keep safe. (Read the information given and it will help you to know what to do.)

a blue rectangle

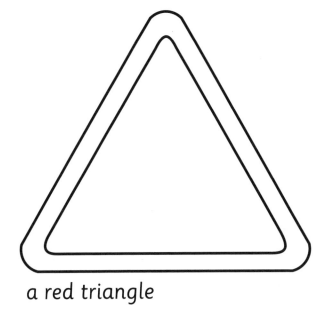

a red triangle

Signs tell us something.

A red circle tells us not to do something.

A red triangle warns us.

A blue rectangle tells us something we need to know.

A green rectangle gives us directions.

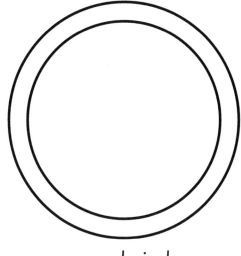

a red circle

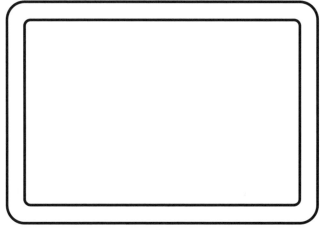

a green rectangle

Crossing the road safely

Name

Read this carefully with your family and practise what it says when you go out with them.

Find a safe place to cross. Do not cross between parked cars.

Stop at the kerb. Use a pelican crossing.

Look right and left and right again. Keep looking both ways.

Listen carefully. You may hear something coming before you see it.

If it is safe, cross quickly to the other side. Keep looking both ways and listening.

Step on to the pavement and away from the kerb. Always keep away from the edge of the pavement.

Early Years: **Look After Yourself**

Play safely

Name

Tick the pictures you think show safe places to play or safe things to play with.
Put a cross by those that are unsafe.

swings

water

kitchen

road

fire

medicines

railway

building sites

strangers

farmyard

television

garden

arly Years: **Look After Yourself**
© 1998 Channel Four Learning Limited

Know How You Feel

Activity sheet 1.
Friends

The activity

If children are to develop high self-esteem they need to understand the importance of valuing oneself and others. Ask them what a friend is. What do they look for in a friend? Invite them to describe their best friend without naming him/her. Can the others guess who it is? Can pets be counted as 'friends'? Give out the activity sheet and, if possible, some mirrors. Tell them to draw a picture of themselves, write their name(s) and say why their friend likes them. They should then draw a picture of their friend and complete the two sentences.

Further activities

The children could write and colour a card for their best friend, saying why they are their best friend.

Activity sheet 2.
I like it when

The activity

Valuing personal experiences helps children to feel good about themselves and others, and raises their self-esteem. Discuss what makes a 'good day' for them. For example, 'When I visit my nan's'. Why does it feel good? Talk about each picture on the activity sheet. Ask them to match the sentences to the pictures. In the last box they should draw a picture of their own and complete the sentence.

Further activities

The children could choose one of the pictures from the activity sheet and write a story around the activity shown.

Activity sheet 3.
Playing together

The activity

Remind the children that friendship and playing together requires co-operation, sharing, giving, taking turns and sometimes losing. In groups, ask them to discuss what is good about having friends and then report back to the class. Be sensitive to children who might not have any friends in the class. Ask the class what they would do if someone did not have any friends. Ask the children to work in pairs on the activity sheet. When they have finished, review the results together and see which pair has come up with the most words.

Further activities

Organise a Friendship Day. Ask the children to see if they can make one new friend for the day. What kind of things would they want to do with their friend?

Activity sheet 4.
I can help

The activity

Recognising emotions is important. Discuss with the children what it is that makes them happy, frightened, sad and angry. In pairs, ask them to tell each other what makes them sad or angry. Their partner then suggests what might be done to overcome these feelings. Ask them to complete the activity sheet.

Further activities

Ask the children to record on a leaf-shaped piece of paper an example of something they can do to make someone in their family or class feel happy. Draw or paint an outline of a tree with branches. Put each 'leaf' paper on a branch of the 'Happiness Tree'.

Activity sheet 5.
Ups and downs

The activity

Talk about times when things go wrong in our lives, such as losing things, arguing and being frightened. All these things influence the way we feel. Usually we can overcome them. Sometimes we need help. Discuss who can help us when things go wrong. How might the children approach a teacher, a parent or a friend for help? When might be a good time to do that and where? Working in pairs, give each pair a copy of the activity sheet and ask them to play the game.

Further activities

On a sheet of paper, ask the children to describe a 'kind helper' in the school who they can turn to when they need help. They might paste their work on to a card and send it as a thank-you message to that person.

Activity sheet 6.
My pet

The activity

Caring for others can give a sense of responsibility and achievement which can lead to positive feelings, self-confidence and high self-esteem. Ask the children what pet(s) they have. What do pets need to be happy and safe? Compare cats, for example, with rabbits, or gerbils with fish. Does their pet need exercise? Give out the activity sheet. If they do not have a pet of their own, they could choose an imaginary one.

Further activities

Invite your local PDSA or someone from a veterinary practice to come and talk to the children about caring for their pets.

Friends

Name

This is a picture of me.

My name is... .

My friend likes me because

....

....

....

This is my friend.

His/Her name is... .

He/she is my friend because

....

....

....

I like it when

Match the pictures with the sentences below. Then make up one of your own.

I like it when ....

I like it when ....

I like it when ....

I like it when ....

I like it when ....

I like it when ....

I do well at school.

I can play with my friends.

I can walk the dog.

my dad reads to me.

I can help my mum wallpaper.

Early Years: **Look After Yourself**

© 1998 Channel Four Learning Limit

Playing together

Work with a partner. See how many smaller words you can make from the letters of the two words *playing together*. When you have finished, complete the sentence at the bottom of the page.

playing together

I liked working with ....

because ....

I can help

Name _____

Read the sentences below. After each one, say who it is about.
Finish the sentence to say what you would do to help.

frightened
Freddy

unhappy
Harjit

angry Alice

sad Susan

She watched Betty stand on her doll and break it.

I think this person is _____.

To help her I would _____.

She saw a poor dog with his paw bandaged.

I think this person is _____.

To help her I would _____.

He guessed that his dad had forgotten his birthday.

I think this person is _____.

To help him I would _____.

It was very dark in his bedroom and he was worried because he
could not find the light.

I think this person is _____.

To help him I would _____.

Early Years: **Look After Yourself**

Ups and downs

Name

Take a coin and tape the number 1 on one side and the number 2 on the other. Take it in turns with a partner to flick the coin. The number it lands on will decide how many moves you can take. The first to reach school is the winner.

My pet

Draw a picture of your pet in the first box and then draw some of the
things you have to do to keep it happy and safe.

My pet is a..................................... . Its name is..................................... .

I love my pet because...................................

....

....

....